A Faith for Tough Times

A FAITH FOR

TOUGH TIMES

by

HARRY EMERSON
FOSDICK

HARPER & BROTHERS, PUBLISHERS
New York

Library of Congress Catalogue Card Number: 52-8471

Contents

Preface

This volume comprises three lectures delivered on the Earl Foundation at the Pacific School of Religion in February, 1952. The convocation in Berkeley included about a thousand ministers and other Christian leaders and, while the public was welcome, it was to this central group I was supposed primarily to speak. I have not shifted the slant of these lectures from their original audience to the "general reader," nor have I changed the direct style of address in which they first were couched. This imposes on the reader of this book—if he is to grasp its purpose and forgive its limitations—the necessity of reading with his ears as well as with his eyes. The direct, colloquial discourse used in these lectures not only presupposes auditors but envisions the particular group of auditors to whom I spoke.

At one point after another in the lectures expansion, interpretation and further argumentation were obviously called for, which the limits of time made impossible. I have resisted the temptation to supply these elaborations in the published book, fearing to produce a hybrid—half address and half treatise. I am trusting my readers to understand what I am driving at, and to accept the inevitable incompleteness of lectures on such themes as I have chosen.

These lectures, of course, do not pretend to cover the whole Christian faith; many factors in our faith, not dealt with here, are profoundly needed in these confusing times; but I hope that some listeners who first heard them and some readers who now peruse them may find in them certain emphases vitally relevant to our generation's spiritual problems.

I am deeply indebted to my hosts at the Pacific School of Religion, who made my stay there an enheartening experience. I shall always retain the grateful memory of their hospitality.

HARRY EMERSON FOSDICK

I

The Eternal Is Real

A disordered generation, such as ours, shakes the confidence of many in religion's basic truths. This confused world can easily be seen as a purposeless welter, with everything pointless and transitory. As in the old story of Sinbad the Sailor, anchoring his boat on what seemed an island, but finding it to be instead a great beast of the sea, that went charging off with him, boat and all, across the tossing ocean, so our trusted stabilities fail, and disturbed societies and nations drag us with them in turmoil. Just such chaotic times as these, however, can light up religious faith's profoundest meaning: its assertion that this fugitive earthly scene is permeated with the eternal; that transiency is not the last word in this universe; that life's changefulness is underlain and penetrated by an unchanging purpose; that behind and within all vicissitude "from everlasting to everlasting" is God.

Certainly, our contemporary world is a mess.

"Everything nailed down is comin' loose," as the Angel Gabriel in *Green Pastures* said to "de Lawd." International relations, economic conditions, moral customs, are inconstant and confused, and such instability unsettles us that Jeremy Taylor's picture of a man clapping his shoulder to the ground to stop an earthquake is understandable by anyone who has labored hard to steady and improve the world. Ideas, habits, institutions, ethical standards, once apparently solid and durable, now seem to many "frail as frost landscapes on a windowpane." The hydrogen bomb makes everything on earth seem perishable, and modern astronomy confirms the ancient Psalmist's condescension to the stars:

Yea, all of them shall wax old like a garment;
As a vesture shalt thou change them, and they
    shall be changed.

This transitory aspect of our world and of our lives within it confronts us all, and to some people the most cogent affirmations, even in our Christian hymns, are lines like

Change and decay in all around I see.

In our vocabulary, however, is another set of words—unchangeable, permanent, eternal. What do such words mean? Can it be that life is not all flux and mutability, fugitive, fleeting, perishing? Is there something else here—abiding, everlasting? That question goes to the very heart of religious faith.

Life on a transient planet, in an exploding universe, with all existence the ephemeral result of colliding physical particles going it blind, is ultimately meaningless. It comes from nowhere and is going nowhither. Its only continuity is the repetition of endless variation; its only changeless element is change. There is no design behind it, no purpose in it, no outcome ahead of it, and Macbeth's description of it is accurate: "full of sound and fury, signifying nothing." Only when amid this jumble of vicissitude and mutability something constant and abiding is seen, only when the eternal emerges amid the transient, is there any ultimate sense in human life, and for the lack of *that* increasing numbers of people are confused and desperate. As one young collegian put it, "What is there to tie to?"

To be sure, many thoughtlessly shrug off serious consideration of life's final significance, and proceed from day to day on what passing happiness they find. But soon or late the ultimate question confronts most of us—what does life mean in a mess of a world like this?—and in these days of upheaval the number of souls facing that question multiplies. Browning, in a burst of optimism, sang:

> God's in his heaven,
> All's right with the world,

but an American soldier changed that second line. "All's riot with the world," he said.

Generations differ in their most urgent needs. History could be written in terms of the varied intellectual and spiritual problems which, from age to age, have pressed up into the crucial focus of attention; and in our time, tottering with world-wide convulsions, this problem which we are considering is importunate. To find the permanent amid the impermanent, the durable amid the fugitive, is now a matter of life and death. Wrote Theodore Dreiser:

> I find life to be not only a complete illusion or mirage which changes and so escapes or eludes one at every point, but the most amazing fanfare of purely temporary and always changing and ever vanishing and, in the main, clownish and ever ridiculous interests that it has ever been my lot to witness. . . . At best, whatever man does is something that can only prolong the struggles and worries and, for the most part, futile dreams of those with whom he finds himself companioned here in this atomic or cellular welter, and which in the last analysis may be just nothing at all—a phantasmagoric or cinematic shadow play.
>
> As I see him, the unutterably infinitesimal individual weaves among the mysteries a floss-like and wholly meaningless course—if course it be. In short, I catch no meaning from all I

have seen, and pass quite as I came, confused
and dismayed.

For such souls, dizzy with life's mutability,
religious faith has salvation to offer. All religions,
in one way or another, have tried to offer it—not
by denying the transiency but by asserting the
eternal too. Shelley faced an awful possibility
when he said, "Nought may endure but Mutability." Religious faith, however, roundly affirms the
contrary. Something else endures—something imperishable, giving point and purpose to creation
and to our lives within it, putting sense and meaning into existence, and even setting folk to saying:

O Thou who changest not, abide with me.

Indeed a chaotic era, such as ours, presents not
only the *need* of discerning the abiding amid the
transitory, but as well the *opportunity* of discerning it. The highest use of a shaken time is to
discover the unshakable. When everything that
can totter is staggering, then is the time to get
our eyes on what stands firm. As Jesus put it in his

parable, two houses, one built on sand and the other on rock, look much alike in tranquil weather. Who can discern the difference between them then? But when the rains descend, the floods come, and the winds blow and beat upon them, then one sees which is solid and which insecure. In a troubled era this is the secret of the soul's triumph—using the shaken time to reveal all the more clearly the unshakable.

Here, as always in our most critical problems, the Bible anticipates us. The Epistle to the Hebrews was written in an era much like ours. The Roman Empire, unifying the known world, had broken through the barricades which hitherto had separated people from people and had kept their pet provincialisms from disturbing contacts. In that age, too, mankind faced "one world"—old nationalisms, politics, racial differences, economies, religions and philosophies poured into one receptacle, tumbled together into a propinquity which meant not peace, but misunderstanding, discord, hatred, war. In particular, the Jews had lost their most cherished securities. Their dearest affections had twined about the Temple. The Temple gone! The central symbol of their worship had been the sacrifices upon Zion. The altars gone! The priesthood had been the venerable medium for their sin's confession and God's returning pardon. The priesthood gone! Everywhere in this epistle one faces the transitory and perishable: "That which is becoming old and waxing aged is nigh unto vanishing away."

One who in a time like that could write a letter worth preserving all these centuries has a message for us. He took advantage of an era when everything else was being shaken to discover what nothing could shake. He used the world's upheaval to distinguish between the solid and the insecure, the substantial and the flimsy, the abiding and the transient. Everywhere the writer's swift and sensitive fingers lay hold on things that last. When he speaks of his hope, it is "an anchor, sure and steadfast." When he talks about his Lord, he is "Jesus Christ, the same yesterday, today and forever." When he interprets his times, he says: "The removing of things that are shaken, that the things which cannot be shaken may remain." And in an era when multitudes were sick with confusion, he took his stand on a firm faith: we have, he said, "a kingdom that cannot be shaken."

In our own way, we to whom Christian faith is real should be doing now what that ancient writer did, and, if we do it well, we shall offer to the hungry the bread they cry for. In one of our colleges, the dean's office discovered that a woman for the last four years had elected the same course in algebra, although she had passed it the first time. The dean, therefore, wrote for an explanation, and the woman replied: "I am so tired of arguing with my neighbors about everything in this world that I wanted to study something I couldn't argue about." Urgent human hunger was speaking there. Wanted: something, even mathematics, that in this perishable world is secure and constant!

As a matter of fact, even in our ordinary experience, despite this earth's impermanence, we do live in two worlds, one transient, the other abiding.

A deeply religious friend of mine was a mathematician and, whenever he talked about religion, his faith seemed rooted in his mathematics. He inhabited two words, one full of fluctuation and change, the other eternal, absolute, its truth true of all worlds and all time. From three times three equals nine up, he moved in at least one realm which was everlastingly so.

Or, read Shakespeare's plays and one runs on customs, circumstances, ways of thinking and speaking so at variance with ours that they loudly advertise the inconstancy of human life. Shakespeare's age is not ours—how all has changed! But then come those passages that have no date— Hamlet facing indecision, Lady Macbeth wrestling with remorse, Portia pleading for mercy—and lo! the centuries vanish, and we confront the timeless, ageless, dateless soul of man. At least some meaning, even though it be limited, inheres in the distinction between the transitory and the abiding.

Or, go to your homes from here by bus, train,

automobile—that is new. Go up to your apartment in an elevator—that is new. See the gadgets with which our modern homes are furnished—they are new. But if you chance to have a copy of Homer's *Odyssey* handy, read this: "There is nothing mightier or nobler than when man and wife are of one heart and mind in a house." Wherever in the universe there may be homes, that is true.

Or, go to sea, and amid the tumult of some oceanic storm, which well may symbolize the age we live in, watch the pilot on the bridge—his eye on the compass, bound by invisible ties to the magnetic pole which no storms can reach. He inhabits two worlds, one tumultuous, the other from age to age the same.

Or, consider history. So much of it is transient! Empires rise and fall, melee follows melee, and everything human seems inconstant. But some things are strangely permanent, anvils that wear out many hammers. The mystery of their continuance is too profound to be superficially brushed off. What is that factor in our evanescent universe, indubitably here though it may seem incredible, which keeps us singing,

> In the cross of Christ I glory,
> Towering o'er the wrecks of time.

Or, read biography. Consider a man like William Penn, facing such vicissitudes of fortune from the dirt and darkness of prisons to the perils of the American wilderness as would have bowled most of us over! Penn, however, had deep within him something that the Bible calls being "builded on a rock," had underneath him what the Bible calls "the everlasting arms," a faith in God and an inner relationship with him which time and tide could not alter, so that at threescore years and ten, he said: "I bless the Lord. I am yet upon my Rock, a lasting foundation."

Say the worst about us mortals, we are still strangely amphibious, inhabiting two worlds, haunted by the consciousness of something durable, changeless, imperishable. In vain we try to live as though only the transient were real, and, despite our own mortality and our world's evanescense, in our ears, as Francis Thompson said,

> . . . ever and anon a trumpet sounds
> from the hid battlements of eternity.

This situation is involved in the very nature of truth. Any fundamental truth, such as that two times two equals four, is everlastingly true. In a scientific age how can men say, as some do, that all is transient, while science so constantly piles up its discoveries not only of contingent facts but of universal laws? There *is* something here on which the tooth of time and the wastage of life's mutability have no effect—truth, at the very least mathematical formulas and cosmic laws which everlastingly are so. But truth is spiritual. It is not a tangible, visible thing. It moves on the nonmetric level, not to be seen, touched, weighed or measured. When Einstein says that a cosmic law is so, his statement moves in the intellectual, spiritual realm where, discovered or undiscovered, there certainly are universal laws, not subject to fortuity and change. Whatever else may be transient, something here is imperishable—everlasting truth.

Even the atheist must accept this affirmation. There is no God, he says; all existence is the accidental by-product of protons and electrons making their undesigned, ephemeral combinations. That is the truth, he says. But, if that is true, it is the everlasting truth. He, too, has unwittingly moved up into the spiritual realm and, amid the purposeless transiency which he affirms, he is affirming also the presence of the eternal. This is a strange universe—on any a priori ground an incredible universe—and at the center of its mystery is human intellect, unable to think at all without thinking about truth and so conceiving and discovering laws which are immutably so. Theist and atheist so far must agree: the eternal is real.

When the Christian, therefore, interprets the

eternal in his special terms, he is interpreting Something which is really here. This explains in part why there are so few thoroughgoing atheists. Deny as they may the Christian interpretation of that eternal Something, they are haunted by the inescapable fact that It is here.

As for Christian faith, it faces, as does the atheist, this huge, weird, mutable universe, where light from the distant nebulae has been traveling over 186,000 miles a second for 140,000,000 years to reach us. Imagination bogles and breaks down trying to conceive the vastness of the cosmos and the making and unmaking of its stellar galaxies. The thought of it can stagger us, bulldoze us into utter insignificance. Are we not complete nonentities in such a cosmos? Then the Christian thinks again. After all, which is more marvelous, more indicative of what ultimate reality is like, the fact that the vast universe so encompasses us, or the fact that man's mind so encompasses the vast universe, measures its distances, plots its laws? This is the critical juncture where man's varied philosophies meet and part, and the affirmation with which theistic faith begins is clear: *the mind that encompasses the universe is more marvelous and revelatory than the universe that encompasses the mind.* That insight opens up a whole world view. Matter, however vast and changeable its manifestations may be, is not central. Said Arthur Balfour, the physicist: "We now know too much about matter to be materialists." The deepest factor in this cosmos which the physical scientist discovers in his research is not physical at all; it is a mathematical formula, and *that* is mental, if anything is. The universe is intelligible; mind fits into it; mind encircles and penetrates it; and mind discovers mental reality waiting to meet it.

There was once a little child who never could get straight the rhyme about "Twinkle, twinkle, little star." He always said it this way:

> Twinkle, twinkle, little star,
> How you wonder what I are.

Man's profoundest philosophies have started with

some such shift of center from the huge and variable universe to the understanding mind. As in the Bethlehem story it was not the child who showed deference to the star, but the star that showed deference to the child, so from Plato on the seers have found in personality the central, revelatory fact; not things understood but the understanding person is the central marvel, interpreting mind meeting in the cosmos Mind waiting to be interpreted. As the opening verses of John's gospel put it, in the best translation I know: "In the beginning was Mind, and the Mind was with God, and the Mind was God."

Our shaken generation profoundly needs the proclamation of that truth. We should be humble, tolerant, open-minded, aware of our limited, fallible knowledge—yes! But, as Gilbert Chesterton said, "I am incurably convinced that the object of opening the mind, as of opening the mouth, is to shut it again on something solid." When the Christian does that, affirming the centrality of Mind as eternal truth, his message becomes rele-

vant to a chaotic time like this, desperately in need
of Arthur Hugh Clough's experience:

> It fortifies my soul to know
> That, though I perish, Truth is so:
> That, howsoe'er I stray and range,
> Whate'er I do, Thou dost not change.
> I steadier step when I recall
> That, if I slip Thou dost not fall.

Christian faith affirms not only eternal truth
but eternal purpose. Mind without purpose is in-
conceivable and, if mind is central in the cosmos,
then creation has significant intent, is moving
toward a designed end or, as the Christian would
declare, is permeated with "the eternal purpose
which He purposed in Christ Jesus our Lord."

This is the very gist of life's problem in multitudes of souls today. The chart of popular optimism carries an unsteady line, and now the drop is
ominous. Fifty years ago hopefulness was easy.
The idea of inevitable progress was in the air. It
was then the hymn was written:

The day of dawning brotherhood
Breaks on our eager eyes,
And human hatreds flee before
The radiant Eastern skies.

This unmitigated optimism is commonly blamed on religious liberals, but its source goes back to men who were not religious at all—to rationalists like Condorcet, Turgot, Proudhon, Comte. It was Condorcet, regarding all religion as irrational superstition, who said, "The perfectibility of man is absolutely indefinite," and, "can never be retrogressive." It was Turgot, friend of Voltaire, refusing holy orders because he could not "bear to wear a mask all his life," who wrote: "The whole mass of humanity . . . marches constantly, though slowly, toward greater perfection." It was Herbert Spencer, the agnostic, who said: "Progress is not an accident, not a thing within human control, but a beneficent necessity . . . due to the working of a universal law. So surely must the things we call evil and immorality disappear; so surely must man become perfect."

These rationalists were in revolt—in revolt, first, against the old idea that the Golden Age was in the past; in revolt, second, against the ancient pagan idea that human history is cyclical, going forever around the same course and repetitiously returning to the place it started; in revolt, third, against primitive Christian ideas that all human hope depends on supernatural interventions in history, as in some messianic reign. They had another concept altogether: that the Golden Age is ahead, inevitably ahead, and that humanity, as though upon an escalator, is willy-nilly being lifted to utopia by universal law. Backed by the rationalists, it was easy then for Christians to believe in God's eternal purpose.

Now, however, such optimism has been shown up as insubstantial folly. Inevitable progress is a flimsy dream. It seems incredible today that in 1913 Walter Rauschenbusch could have said: "The larger part of the task of Christianizing our social order is already accomplished." And with the collapse of that superstructure of exuberant optimism, hope has come tumbling down, and faith in God's eternal purpose has in multitudes been shaken to its foundations.

It is not within our present scope to argue the case for a purposeful universe, but this much is relevant to our intent: in a time like this, when insubstantial optimisms have collapsed, convinced Christians should all the more firmly grasp their conviction concerning God's eternal purpose. Our mid-Victorian optimism has collapsed because it deserved to collapse. It took too little account of human sin and stupidity. It was based on fallacious ideas, such as that the new science, mastering nature and opening channels of world-wide inter-communication to all mankind, would straightway usher in the reign of brotherhood and peace. The fallibility of a flimsy optimism, however, is no excuse for surrendering the assurance of an eternal purpose. Our choice is not restricted to gullible optimism, on one side, and, on the other, von Hartmann's dictum that "the activities of the busy world are only the shudderings of a fever." Beneath

the ups and downs of transient popular hopefulness and despair an abiding purpose may still be
holding history together. Still beneath these flooded
plains there may be a central river bed, and a river
which came from somewhere and is going some-
whither. Such is the Christian's conviction, seen
all the more clearly, held all the more stoutly, because superficial optimisms which deserved to fall
have fallen.

Here, too, the Bible anticipates our problem.
The thirteenth chapter of First Corinthians is
commonly regarded as a poem about love, but it
is more than that—a statement of Paul's distinction
between the fleeting and the abiding. Prophecies,
says Paul, they shall fail; tongues, they shall cease;
knowledge, it shall vanish away; that which is in
part shall be done away, he says; when I became a
man I put away childish things. Throughout the
chapter he is dealing with the transitory aspects of
this mortal life, but then come two resounding
words: *"Now abideth."* The perennial is here, he
says, amid the flux. We can get our eyes upon it

now. We can build our lives upon it. We need not live merely in a world of mutability. "Now abideth faith, hope, love"—faith in the sovereign God, hope in his eternal purpose, love that "suffereth long, and is kind."

That message is profoundly needed in this generation. If this universe, having developed personality with all its possibilities, were merely the work of purposeless chance, it would be insane, as many who hold that theory say it is. To be sure, a few others positively rejoice in a meaningless world, because it relieves them of personal responsibility. "No dashing around," writes one atheist, delighting in the consequences of his creed; "no dashing around hunting for a point or purpose in your life! There is no point or purpose." And still others, accepting random chance as the universe's explanation, resolve that nonetheless they themselves will be purposeful, serving noble aims in an aimless world. Thus making the best of a bad mess, however, leaves out of account a vast range of facts, so indicative of order, law-abidingness, progress, meaning, purpose, that one anthropologist's exclamation, "I cannot accept chaos," is echoed by most serious thinkers. Despite chaotic days, something is significantly afoot in creation. As William James wrote: "If this life be not a real fight, in which something is eternally gained for the universe by success, it is no better than a game of private theatricals from which one may withdraw at will. But it *feels* like a real fight." With a psychologist's restraint James was saying there what the Christian should proclaim with convincing power, that the eternal truth about this universe involves an eternal purpose.

Moreover, eternal truth, interpreted in terms of eternal purpose, involves eternal moral law. "History," said Mommsen, "has a Nemesis for every sin." Is that really true—everlasting standards of right and wrong; an ultimate tribunal where good and evil, justice and iniquity, are judged; this universe governed not by physical law alone, but by moral law as well?

Upon the contrary, to many nothing seems more fluctuating and unstable than moral standards. Are they not all relative? Ethical customs and demands are geographically bounded, men say, and what is right here is wrong somewhere else. It is all like Jews wearing their hats in synagogue and Christians doffing their hats in church—a mere convention. What each nation, race, religion thinks determines for them right and wrong, as though each could regulate his own watch and there were no such thing as sun time. Nothing is more disintegrating to character in these troubled times than such ethical bewilderment. Life is like a football game. Back and forth, up and down the field, the strenuous game progresses, and sometimes in a tangled mass the players pile together in confusion. But not everything in a football game is thus changeful; the goal posts are not unsteady; they are set. In the jargon of the schools they are the "frame of reference" in which the game is played. What a football game would be without goal posts, life would be without moral standards. Is that the real situation?

As a matter of fact, in our serious hours we do not believe such ethical cynicism. Granted the endless variations of moral customs, still the essential standards persist. As in a scientific laboratory, all else may change but the *standards* are unalterable—disinterested love of truth, fidelity to facts, accuracy in measurement, exactness of verification—so, in life as a whole, the towering ethical criteria remain unshaken. Falsehood is never better than truth, theft better than honesty, treachery better than loyalty, cowardice better than courage. As James Russell Lowell said:

> In vain we call old notions fudge,
> And bend our conscience to our dealing;
> The Ten Commandments will not budge,
> And stealing will continue stealing.

In the midst of his desperate struggle for a Christian faith, Frederick W. Robertson, the English preacher, wrote this:

> In the darkest hour through which a human soul can pass, whatever else is doubtful, this at least is certain. If there be no God and no future

state, yet, even then, it is better to be generous than selfish, better to be chaste than licentious, better to be true than false, better to be brave than to be a coward. Blessed beyond all earthly blessedness is the man who, in the tempestuous darkness of the soul, has dared to hold fast to these venerable landmarks. Thrice blest is he who, when all is drear and cheerless within and without, when his teachers terrify him, and his friends shrink from him, has obstinately clung to moral good.

Quote that anywhere on earth, and men and women of rectitude and intelligence, whose judgment you would trust, will understand and respond.

Moreover, beyond this relative permanence of great ethical standards despite kaleidoscopic changes of habit and custom, there are facts indicative of cosmic moral law. The law-abidingness of this cosmos does not stop at the frontier of the physical; it carries over into the moral world. How typical of human history is Belshazzar's feast! The bloody and insensate conquerer spread a banquet for a thousand of his lords, and the captured vessels from the house of God which had been in Jerusalem were brought before him, that the king and his princes, his wives and his concubines, might drink therefrom; and then, when pride and sacrilege were at their height, out of the unseen came fingers, writing on the wall, MENE, MENE, TEKEL, UPHARSIN—"Thou art weighed in the balances, and art found wanting"—and the king's "knees smote one against another." That scene represents a fact in this universe: an ultimate justice, a final court of arbitrament, a tribunal greater than our own, the God of moral law sitting king even at the Flood.

Indeed, our present chaos, far from refuting, bears witness to such inexorable laws in the ethical realm, with which we have been trifling. We are like a man who has walked out of a third-story window and then complains that he is badly shaken. He is shaken because he has transgressed laws that are unshakable. Consider, then, what the last generation has been doing—our wars, our militant nationalisms, our imperialistic greed, our racial discrimination, our economic avarice, our dedication of science to destructive purposes! We are shaken because there are unshakable moral laws with which men and nations may not innocuously fool.

We commonly take comfort from this fact of cosmic moral law. The Hitlers and Mussolinis do not get away with it. A tyrant, like Stalin, will not get away with it—not in the long run. They are up against something inexorable in the cosmos— the moral law. So Victor Hugo attributed Napoleon's downfall to more than mortal man; as Hugo put it, Napoleon "bothered God." Not simply encouraging, however, the morally law-abiding nature of the cosmos is as well ominous, threatening, as the Bible insists. It confronts every man and woman, saying: Stop talking as though everything were chaotic and changeable; you deceive yourselves; you can as easily escape gravitation as you can evade the silent, relentless operation of moral law; *you* cannot get away with it either! "Whatsoever a man soweth, that shall he also reap," is an everlasting fact.

Eternal truth, eternal purpose, eternal moral law—all three are basic to the Christian gospel, but they are not the gospel. The Christian faith makes another affirmation: a personality is abiding, Jesus Christ, "the same yesterday, today and forever." He incarnates the truth; he personifies the purpose; he embodies the moral law; and, beyond all that, he reveals what only personality can reveal—the imperishable grace and love of God. It is an astounding assertion. To it in these lectures we shall repeatedly return, but now, for a moment, we stand before it in amazement. Into a world of ghastly immediacies Christ came, and he has outlived them all. Caesar and his empire, the Roman legions and their wars, have passed, and still unshaken, abidingly to be returned to from mankind's long detours, he stands. When one undertakes to find the permanent in this transitory world one naturally turns to huge things, powerful things, which ostentatiously loom large and dominate the scene. But the Christian faith lights on an obscure Galilean, whose family thought him demented, whose church thought him a heretic and excommunicated him, whose friends thought him a failure and disowned him, whose nation thought him a traitor and crucified him. He lasts when all else passes, says Christian faith—his truth everlastingly so, his ideals the pillar of cloud by day and of fire by night, his spirit the revelation of eternal God. Is not this utterly incredible? And yet, what is it in this universe which continually confirms the Christian insight?

> The tumult and the shouting dies;
> The captains and the kings depart—
> Still stands Thine ancient Sacrifice,
> An humble and a contrite heart.[1]

[1] Rudyard Kipling, "Recessional," from *The Five Nations.* Copyright, 1910, by Rudyard Kipling; reprinted with permission of Mrs. George Bambridge, Doubleday & Company, Inc., and the Macmillan Company of Canada, Ltd.

At any rate Jesus is a fact, and a fact is always more than a fact—it is a revelation. Seen with discerning eyes a common fact, like Newton's falling apple, may unveil universal laws and truths, which are the stuff of the cosmos. Materialists hold that only physical facts are thus revelatory, that persons are accidents. It will not do! The chance of that's being true, says one modern philosopher, would have to be represented by a fraction with one for the numerator, and a denominator that would reach from here to the fixed stars. Mind, spirit, personal character also come from Reality and disclose its nature. Christian faith is not irrational when it holds that Jesus is a supremely revelatory fact.

He reveals human nature, as it was never revealed before—undoubtedly wicked, vicious, depraved, monstrously sinful—but with something profounder there too: a divine light, lighting every man coming into the world, a soul whose kinship with goodness cannot be utterly obliterated, a capacity for loving the highest when he sees it, for

contrition, pardon, spiritual rebirth, ethical hero-
ism, communion with God and loyal obedience
to his will. He reveals ethical standards, concerning which in this violent world, committing suicide
with its selfishness and ill will, we are compelled
repeatedly to say, despite our cynicism and incredulity, that he is everlastingly right. And he reveals
God, the only kind of God who can be deity in a
world of eternal truth, purposefulness and moral
law. A young British lad, whose father had been
long away from home during the war, stood in
front of his father's picture, and said to his mother,
"I wish that father could step out the the frame."
As Christian faith sees it, God in Christ did step
out of the frame, made himself manifest, so that
when we say "God," we mean something definite
and describable, and when we believe in God, we
believe in someone real and commanding.

We need not identify that truth with all the
complicated and often incredible theology which
has been associated with it. We may readily grant
that while there are absolutes, nevertheless when-

ever an absolute comes in contact with a human mind it becomes relative—relative to the limitations of conception, the frailties of imagination, the inadequacies of vocabulary, which beset our human intellects. Nonetheless the Christian affirmation is clear and confident: Jesus Christ is in our world the supremely revelatory Fact, unveiling what everlastingly is so.

In speaking thus of the reality of the eternal, we have not mentioned immortality. Immortality is a corollary—an inevitable corollary of such a world view as we have presented—but unless one sees the eternal permeating this present world, post-mortem everlastingness lacks sense and meaning. Here and now we deal with the permanent and imperishable. Here and now we can discover what neither moth nor rust consume nor thieves break through and steal. And that discovery brings with it a spiritual victory which our generation desperately needs. No longer are we the victims of chaos and fortuity. No longer is change merely an enemy to be feared. The world needs to be changed! Change is an inevitable factor in a cosmos where eternal truth, expressed in eternal purpose and abiding moral law, is working out the principles revealed in a personality like Christ. The whole tone of a man's life now shifts from the defensive to the offensive. Change is his special *forte*, his ideal and his obligation. A changeless universe would be static; only an endlessly changeable world has hope. The very mutability which once confused him now challenges him, and he may even find himself quoting with elation:

> Time makes ancient good uncouth;
> They must upward still, and onward,
> Who would keep abreast of Truth.

Such is the Christian's victory in an upset world. We have indeed a faith for tough times—"while we look not at the things which are seen, but at the things which are not seen: for the things which are seen are temporal; but the things which are not seen are eternal."

II

Vitality Is Mightier
Than Size

We human beings are obsessed by size. Samuel Goldwyn once remarked that he wanted a "film which begins with an earthquake and works up to a climax." He rightly assessed the popular attractiveness of the colossal. If, however, one's thinking is dominated by the gigantic events of our time, one can hardly avoid despair. The world's spectacular doings are in turmoil. As George Bernard Shaw said, if the other planets are inhabited they must be using this earth as their insane asylum.

Christian faith maintains its assurance, despite the world's disorder, by centering attention on something else here, not vast or noisy, but quiet, unobtrusive, inconspicuous, vital. Jesus pictured his own reliance on this truth when he compared the kingdom of heaven to "leaven, which a woman took and hid in three measures of meal, till it was all leavened." The lump and the leaven—with which of these two popular thinking is naturally obsessed, there is no doubt. The huge lump of the world is spectacular; filled with noisy tumult, it blatantly demands attention; but, if one sees only that, there is little hope. Something else, however, is here, says Jesus, inconspicuous, reticent, vital. Mass is not the whole story; invisible leaven is at work, with the question rising whether we shall believe that bulk and size are decisive or that, in the long run, leaven can win.

Every Christmas we celebrate this truth. How irrelevant to the vast affairs of the Roman world seemed the birth of a baby in the inn! Gigantic events were afoot then, and here was

> . . . a little baby thing
> That made a woman cry.

Yet empires fell, the Caesars are dust, the spectacular affairs which then had bulk and magnitude in the world's opinion have proved transient, and that diminutive bit of vitality has proved more enduring than them all. No wonder that William James, impatient with the worship of size, exclaimed:

Vitality Is Mightier Than Size

As for me, my bed is made. I am against big-ness and greatness in all their forms, and with the invisible, molecular moral forces that work from individual to individual, stealing in through the crannies of the world like so many soft rootlets, or like the capillary oozing of water, and yet rending the hardest monuments of man's pride, if you give them time.

If this seems sentimental, imagine yourselves back some millions of years ago on this planet, facing two factors here: on one side, a vast turbu-lence—volcanoes, huge, terrific, from the inex-haustible fires of the earth's core; on the other side, protoplasm, microscopic, invisible along the water's edge, fragile, quiet, vital. On which are we betting as, in imagination, we stand there millions of years ago—volcanoes or protoplasm? Proto-plasm had no credible chance to mean anything as against the violent forces of volcano and earth-quake. Yet see what came of it at last: life, spirit, art, music, prophets, apostles, martyrs, scientists and saints! The utterly unforeseeable, the un-

51

imaginable did happen. Vitality *is* mightier than size.

This creative power of the vital is a momentous fact in human history. It explains, at least in part, the striking contrast between the estimates of stormy generations by their contemporaries and by their posterity. In retrospect, as Victor Hugo reminded us, we now see the sixteenth century as a stirring, hopeful time, with the towering figures of the Reformation achieving liberties in which we glory yet; but, had we ourselves lived then, many of us would not have felt that. Even Erasmus, sympathetic though he was with much that was afoot, called that era "the excrement of the ages." In retrospect the seventeenth century appears to us as a marvelous epoch, opening up the new world with its venturesome discoveries, so that many of us are here now because our ancestors in that formidable time dared the Atlantic's crossing to settle in this new land; but, had we ourselves lived then, we might not so have valued it. Bossuet, who did live then, called it "a wicked and paltry age." In retrospect the eighteenth century, with its American and French Revolutions, appears to us one of the most creative in history; but many who lived then never guessed that posterity would so regard it. Even Rousseau called it "this great rottenness amidst which we live." In those stormy eras something momentous was afoot, not obvious to superficial observance, not easily discernible amid the noise, but germinative, creative, decisive. So, today, many look on our generation with hopeless eyes but, if we have anything like the faith and character of our forefathers at their best, our posterity, looking back, will sometime wonder why we, who had the privilege of living now, did not better understand that we were

> . . . dwelling
> In a grand and awful time,
> In an age on ages telling;
> To be living is sublime.

This difference between contemporaries and their progeny in estimating revolutionary eras finds its major explanation in the contrast with which we are dealing. Center attention on the ostentatious events in any age, and one can easily regard the epoch with disdain and disheartenment. In every such era, however, the most rememberable factors turn out to be not the vociferous affairs which split the eardrums of contemporaries, but vital forces, embryonic, secretive, often imperceptible to the majority. Contemporaries miss them; to posterity they are the outstanding, creative facts.

As for our generation, of course it is in turmoil. Not long ago nations, races and religions, fairly well pocketed and capsuled by geographical isolation, could live each for itself, so that the idea of one world was a dream; but now suddenly we have all been poured into one container, distance conquered, so that what happens anywhere happens everywhere. Optimists foresaw world brotherhood as the immediate result of this new propinquity. Of course not—friction, turmoil, confusion, misunderstanding, hatred, war! We shall not get out of this mess in a hurry. We are in for an uproarious era. That, however, is not the whole truth. The abiding, creative factors in this revolutionary time are its vitalities. The lump is massive, its condition crude, but the leaven is here too. Indeed, the leaven in no small measure causes the disturbance. It will not let the lump alone. Not man's wickedness only, but man's ideals, his ethical protests, his just demands for life, liberty and the pursuit of happiness, his revolutionary endeavors to better his condition, upset the world, so that not serene generations but times of tumult, when outward circumstance and inward fermentation have perturbed mankind, have always been the creative epochs in human history. Our generation will yet be seen by our progeny as one world painfully in the making. As Professor Whitehead of Harvard said, the great ages in history have always been the unstable ages.

The Christian gospel has many ministries to offer in a time like this, but none more needed than its faith in the spiritual vitalities which the multitude commonly misses. These vital truths and ideals are not momentary bubbles, as the cynics think, but creative forces by which our children will estimate the greatness of our era. So Nebuchadnezzar once ruled the world, and Jeremiah was a defeated prophet. But now—who was Nebuchadnezzar, no sooner victorious than his empire fell, nothing left of him for ages except a cruel name, a few clay tablets and ruins where jackals dwell? In Jeremiah, however, was power whose issue Nebuchadnezzar could not have understood: vital, leavening power, that even yet makes his generation rememberable.

This truth is illustrated in vital persons. The history of mankind is pretty much the story of dough, into which the leaven of personality is introduced, with consequences none could have foreseen. This last generation has been fed—not to say, fed up—with deterministic thinking, as though the vast forces of the external world, working through environment and heredity, predetermine all we are and do, so that we are only autoᴍata they push about, Charlie McCarthys they speak through. This kind of deterministic doctrine has been thought scientific, but does not the history of science itself furnish its refutation? The progress of science is inexplicable without the creative impact of vital persons. Here was the dull, sodden mass of man's thinking, and then a person came, unknown, unrecognized, often derided, but vital. Men denied his truth and fought against it. The dough said it would have none of the leaven, but at last Galileo, Darwin, Einstein win.

Some time since I sat with a group of medical research scientists talking about one of their comrades, recently deceased. They spoke of his zeal for truth and of his competence as a scientist; they spoke of the opposition and incredulity he had met and of his courage in facing it, until one of the group said this: "He was wrong for so long, and then he turned out to be right." Probably the speaker has forgotten he said that, but I have not been able to forget it, because it sums up so much human history—a vital person, confronting the massed resistance of the world, wrong for so long, and then he turns out to be right.

At least that much faith in Christ the church should proclaim now wtih conviction and power. Men say that Christ was a dreamer, that his beautiful but impractical ideas will never work, that he was utopian, sentimental, and—most damning adjective of all—unrealistic. Look at this lump of the world, they say; his way of life can never be dominant *here*. So we go on serving anti-Christ. In our wars, our imperialism and colonialism, our racial discrimination and economic exploitation, with our H-bombs and our propaganda of fear and hatred, we follow anti-Christ. But see where that has landed us! See to what deeper abysses of hell it now is leading us! Is all this practical? In terms of the most hardheaded, prudential considerations is anti-Christ proving to be realistic? It is not a preacher but a professor of sociology at Harvard who writes: "There must be a change of the whole mentality and attitudes of our day, in the direction of the norms prescribed in the Sermon on the

Mount." So, by the very test of practicality, which anti-Christ proposes, anti-Christ stands condemned. One Christian affirmation at least I find myself believing now with crucial need and deep conviction: Someday men will be saying about Christ's essential teaching, "He was wrong for so long, and then he turned out to be right."

The story of Sir Isaac Newton reminds one not a little of the world's reception of Jesus. When Newton announced the law of gravitation, one man said that he had a "deranged poetical fancy." Another critic said, "This crazy mathematician will not have twenty followers in his lifetime." Such derision seemed well-founded. Newton met disheartening opposition, so that once he wrote: "I see a man must either resolve to put out nothing new or to become a slave to defend it." Then, however, he began to win until the whole world now understands that his revelation is not deranged poetical fancy but fact, amazing fact and cosmic law.

We are dealing here with one of the most

momentous elements in human history—the inconspicuous emergence of prophetic facts. Once on this planet there was only one form of life, one-celled creatures in the slime along the ocean's shore but, looking back on that so small beginning, we see it now as a prophetic fact. Once there occurred the first emergence of what could be called a human mind but, dim as that dawning intelligence was, it was a prophetic fact. Once, some five thousand years ago, there first appeared what could be called a social conscience, its earliest expressions still preserved in Egypt's ancient records but, hesitant and uncertain as that social conscience was, who can measure the significance of that prophetic fact? Once mankind thought that the sun revolved about the earth, but then Copernicus came, and in one mind and those it influenced dawned a new way of thinking, and that was a prophetic fact.

This is the way the world runs. Always the new beginnings to which the future belongs are born, as it were, in a manger, their prophetic import seen by none save three wise men, it may be, and a few

shepherds. If, therefore, we believe in the noisy
and ostentatious, as though they were the deter-
mining factors, we miss the most important truth
about any era. The wise men believed in a baby—
that is one of the most significant insights in the
Christian record. Wise men? we are tempted to
say; rather fools and sentimentalists to do that!
But what those wise men did is a parable of mankind's best wisdom in every realm. They did not
believe in Herod, in Caesar's legions, in the im-
perial power that loomed large and filled the eyes
and ears of their generation. They believed in
something newborn and vital.

If someone says that it requires amazing faith to
do that, I answer that it requires more than faith.
It takes first-class intelligence to recognize the
emergence of vital persons, incarnating truth
which, thought wrong for centuries, will yet turn
out to be right. It requires intelligence to welcome
Copernicus, Darwin, Pasteur, to accept at their
first appearance the trail blazers and pioneers in
any realm. So in our acceptance of Christ, not

faith alone, certainly not credulity, but perceptive insight is called for. He is, in very truth, a prophetic fact and, amid the huge, vociferous events of our time, he illustrates the abiding verity that vitality is mightier than size.

No wonder the Cinderella theme is endlessly attractive! It symbolizes one of the most constantly repeated events in history—the triumph of rejected persons. As Dr. Moffatt translates the Psalmist:

> The stone the builders cast aside
> Is now the building's strength and pride.

A believer in democracy was once a Cinderella. Our Founding Fathers risked a republic here, but most of them despised democracy. This rabble, this vulgar, illiterate mob were not to be trusted to determine the great affairs of state. John Adams, the first Vice-President of this nation, wrote: "Democracy never has been and never can be so desirable as aristocracy or monarchy; but, while it lasts, is more bloody than either. . . . Remember," he added, "democracy never lasts long. It soon wastes, exhausts and murders itself." Today, however, while democracy is very faulty, it is clear that if human dignity is to be preserved, if essential liberties are to be maintained, if mankind is to go forward not backward, democracy is our hope. No totalitarian system can be trusted now. Ah, Cinderella, our princess now, concerning whom only a neglected minority once supposed that the crystal slipper would ever fit your foot, you symbolize a truth which today cries for our perception!

This triumph of rejected persons is dramatically evident in Christ.

> The Head that once was crowned with thorns
> Is crowned with glory now . . .

so we Christians sing. But how incredible it is that we should sing it! Think your way back to that scene in Pilate's court, and how unbelievable such a hymn is! Look at that thorn-crowned Galilean confronting the Roman procurator! He never will be crowned with glory. No! He is

finished. Mocked and spit upon, flogged and crucified, he is done for. That is the kind of world this
is: man slays his best, and wrong triumphs. Yet,
incredible as it is,

> The head that once was crowned with thorns
> Is crowned with glory now;
> A royal diadem adorns
> The mighty Victor's brow.

That is neither dream nor dogma, but historic fact.
Caesars fall, empires crash and crumble, dictators
are doomed and damned, but vitality is mightier
than size.

As for us as individuals, often seeming power-
less in a mad world, the Christian gospel brings to
us a message, challenging even when it seems
incredible. Vital persons count. Men and women
of integrity and rectitude are "the strong nails that
hold the world together." We never see the truth
in history or in contemporary life until we pierce
behind the mass and bulk of huge affairs and
recognize the momentous importance of individuals. The vast forest depends upon the vitality of

its individual trees. The over-all government of a nation in the long run can do no more than express the quality of its individual citizens. As another put it, "No possible rearrangement of bad eggs can ever make a good omelet." The world's destiny is ultimately determined inside personality.

Our truth holds good with regard not only to vital persons but to vital ideas. Benjamin Franklin, when asked about his new discovery concerning electricity, "What good is it anyway?" retorted: "What good is a newborn baby?" Franklin had a germinative idea, bound to grow, and he staked his faith on it against a whole world's apathy.

I never read the Declaration of Independence without marveling at one sentence in it: "We hold these truths to be self-evident." Then the Declaration rehearses self-evident ideas that for centuries had been derided by all the big forces in the world—that all men are created equal, that they are endowed by their Creator with certain unalienable rights, and so on. Was there ever a set of ideas which for so long were only the tiniest of leaven, the most infinitesimal of seed? Then their day came, when they could be proclaimed as "self-evident."

Great ideas never come into the world full-armored like Minerva from the head of Jove. All saving ideas are born small. In every generation, therefore, if we are to apprehend the abiding forces which will dominate the future, we must believe in something germinative, often diminutive, inconspicuous, like mustard seed, as Jesus said. This is difficult for us humans to do—to see that the show under the big tent does not matter most or last longest. Nevertheless, Victor Hugo was everlastingly right: "Nothing in this world is so powerful as an idea whose time has come."

In that first year of the Peninsular War, when Napoleon's shadow darkened all Europe, what difference did it make that Beethoven wrote his Fifth Symphony? In the summer when Waterloo was fought, what difference did it make that Keats wrote:

Then felt I like some watcher of the skies
When a new planet swims into his ken.

In that tremendous epoch, the world clamorous
with big events, when the Emperor summoned a
little monk from Wittenberg to Worms to answer
for his heresy, what difference did it make that
Luther wrote:

A mighty fortress is our God,
A bulwark never failing.

That day when Caesar bestrode the earth, what
difference did it make that an unknown Jew, con-
verted to a despised cult, wrote the thirteenth
chapter of First Corinthians? Yet now Napoleon
and Waterloo are historic episodes, but the Fifth
Symphony and Keats' poetry are not. Now Luther's
emperor, with all his realm, has vanished, but
Luther's hymn lives on. As for the thirteenth
chapter of First Corinthians,

Imperious Caesar, dead and turn'd to clay,
Might stop a hole to keep the wind away,

but Paul's truth will not down.

One can without difficulty see *in retrospect* this fragility of the big and this persistence of the vital.

> The great god Ra, whose shrines once covered acres,
> Is filler now for crossword puzzle makers.

One can see that in retrospect. But when the great god Ra holds the center of the stage and is making all the noise, it is not easy to perceive that the things seen are temporal, and the things unseen eternal. Yet that insight is the very substance of Christian faith.

We are not saying that the large matters of the world—its politics and wars, its economic systems, its national and international affairs—are unimportant. That would be gross misunderstanding of our truth. When Jesus told his parable about the leaven and the three measures of meal, his final emphasis was not upon the leaven, but upon the transforming effect which the leaven would have upon the whole lump—"until it was all leavened." The big affairs of the world are important—the final objective of every vital person and every saving idea. But it is the vital persons and the saving ideas which must be recognized, believed in and served, if the world as a whole is to be redeemed.

Such is our faith about Christ's ideas, and their relevance to our world's problems. They are only leaven now, most of the meal untouched by their fermentation, but they are at work. Cannot we see *that* even concerning war? "All they that take the sword shall perish with the sword," he said. Is he right or wrong? Mankind for so long has taken war for granted, regarded it as inevitable, even glorified it. As a high school student, I heard Judge Tourgée, a noted novelist and public leader of the time, say in a school assembly. "Every nation needs a good war about once every thirty years." Such a sentiment had behind it, then, both ancient tradition and popular acceptance. Did not Shakespeare's Othello talk about the "Pride, pomp and circumstance of glorious war"? Did not Wilhelm von Humboldt say that the effect of war upon national character is "one of the most salutary ele-

ments in the molding of the race"? Today, however, try telling that to some G. I. fresh from Korea
and see if his remarks are quotable in the *Ladies'
Home Journal*! You recall the two cats of Kil-
kenny:

> Each thought there was one cat too many;
> So they fought and they spit,
> And they scratched and they bit,
> Till, excepting their nails
> And the tips of their tails,
> Instead of two cats, there weren't any.

Such is the realistic fact about war's suicidal
nature, as we see it now. Says General Dwight
Eisenhower, "War is the greatest of social dis-
eases." Says General Douglas MacArthur, "With
present weapons there no longer is any advantage
to winning a war. Everyone loses, with the victor
only losing a little less than the vanquished." Says
General H. H. Arnold, "One nation cannot defeat
another nation today. That concept died with
Hiroshima. War is like fire; you can prevent a
fire or you can try to put it out, but you can't win

a fire, because fire is destruction." Says General
Omar Bradley: "The way to win an atomic war
is to make certain it never starts." During the last
half-century something momentous has been hap-
pening in man's thinking about war. On one side
is the fermentation of ideas: that war is wrong,
that its causes, processes and results are utterly
irreconcilable with Christian principles, that Christ
and war stand in unappeasable contradiction. On
the other side are realistic facts: the destructive
world-wide impact of war on an earth where
distance has been conquered; the invention of new
weapons for mass slaughter; the inevitable involve-
ment in war, not of armies only but of whole
populations; the unavoidable result of such war,
creating worse problems than it solves. This is our
situation today—the realistic facts pushing us in
the same direction in which our ideals are pulling
us, toward the recognition of war as insane, wicked,
suicidal. All man's major social achievements have
come when that conjunction has occurred, when
the *pull* of ideals was backed by the *push* of real-

istic facts. At that point, where the pull of what ideally is right and the push of what realistically is so join forces, there is always tumult but always hope. At that point we are living now. Ours is a great era, the perils terrific but the possibilities momentous. As Reinhold Niebuhr remarked to me: "If you will be a pessimist with me decade by decade, I will be an optimist with you aeon by aeon." As for war, while we may not see the issue of this generation's struggle, our offspring will; and of the "Prince of Peace" mankind will yet be saying, "He was wrong for so long, and then he turned out to be right."

Our truth holds good, not only of vital persons and ideas, but of vital groups. Around Jesus a few disciples gathered, and what an insignificant company they were! What importance had that small circle of fishermen and the like in comparison with the weighty councils of the empire, deciding the world's great affairs? All the miracle stories

told by man's excited and superstitious imagination do not equal this real miracle of history—the
incredible result of the leaven which Jesus planted
in that little company of his disciples.

The dismaying aspect of the world's large affairs
makes all the more important the vital groups—
homes, friendships, neighborhoods, churches—
where the leaven of decency, kindness, good will,
love, has got its start. Small they are, but they are
like hothouses, where slender growths begin which
later can be transplanted to the wider field. This
lump of a world is evil enough, even with this
leaven in it, but what would it be without the
leaven?

Our homes, for example—how much depends
on them can hardly be exaggerated. The family
counts. It is humanity's primary cell. If a nation's
homes disintegrate, nothing can be right. The
United Nations is of superlative importance, but
if the United Nations wins the day for a peaceful
world, that victory will go back to homes where
intelligence, integrity, goodwill and leadership

73

had their vital start. "It All Depends on Our Homes"—so one journalist entitles his statement of concern about our families. Call that exaggeration, if you will, but the fact remains that the world never gets a Christ, or anyone Christlike, except through a Holy Family.

So long as there are homes to which men turn
At the close of day,
So long as there are homes where children are—
Where women stay,
If love and loyalty and faith be found
Across those sills,
A stricken nation can recover from
Its greatest ills.

So long as there are homes where fires burn
And there is bread,
So long as there are homes where lamps are lit
And prayers are said;
Although a people falters through the dark
And nations grope,
With God himself back of these little homes
We still can hope.[1]

[1] Grace Noll Crowell, "So Long As There Are Homes," from *Light of the Years*. Copyright, 1936, by Harper & Brothers and reprinted with their permission.

One of the tragedies of our time is that so many people, obsessed by size, dispirited by the world's chaos, lose heart, throw up the sponge and relax their loyalty to the vital groups. If the earth's large affairs are hellish, they think, what can a small fellowship do? We need the Master's faith in a mustard seed, and nowhere do we need it more than in our churches. It is not their size that matters so much as their vitality. No apostasy, no abandonment of everything Christ stood for, can be much more utter and complete than empty formalism, dry-as-dust ecclesiastical conventionality, torpid routine observance and ceremoniousness. History shockingly reveals this dereliction of religion into lifeless formality, and on this besetting sin Jesus, despite his mercy, visited merciless condemnation. William Watson's stinging lines about the inert, inanimate church stand in the tradition, not of anti-Christianity, but of Christ himself:

> Outwardly splendid, as of old—
> Inwardly sparkless, void and cold—

Her force and fire all spent and gone—
Like the dead moon, she still shines on.[2]

A living church, however, has been and can be still a vital group. When we so think of her, we are not thinking of huge organizations, of prelacies and hierarchies, but of the church within the church, the creative minority whose faith is not merely inherited or borrowed but personally experienced, of the *ecclesia*—souls called out by the grace of God to be in the world but not of it. The churches have achieved bigness also, and "jumbo-ism," the worship of size, can curse them too but, when it does, the church's mission and its great tradition are forgotten. The fellowship of Christ's disciples did not start as a huge organization; it started as leaven. Jesus did not call his followers doctor, priest, bishop; he called them the "seed of the kingdom." And still, at its best, the church proclaims a living gospel which this huge, noisy, violent world critically needs.

[2] "The Church Today," from *The Poems of Sir William Watson 1878-1935*. Reprinted with permission of George G. Harrap & Co., Ltd. and Lady Watson.

Many today think that they are getting on very well without the church, but have they ever pictured realistically what getting on without the church would mean? Let the church die, let generation after generation rise that never knew it, let Jesus become a myth, the Bible's message forgotten, faith in God vague and nebulous, worship finished, no more sacred music—only secular, no more religious education of the children—only secular, a literature from which have been deleted the ideas and ideals that have their rootage in the Christian heritage, and all the leaven gone which the prophets implanted in our race—then we could live without the church. Who wants to try?

Granted the glaring faults of the church, the living gospel is too much alive for any church's failures utterly to deaden it. Despite our deficiencies, still in our churches at their best, lives are transformed, character is built, courage is renewed, faith is strengthened, ideals of personal and social conduct which else would die are kept alive, public-spirited devotion is engendered, and God's kingdom of righteousness on earth is made a living hope. The church, too, illustrates our theme that vital groups are indispensable leaven in a naughty world.

This message concerning the importance of vitality as over against size is the more needed in our time because so many of the reliances in which we trusted have failed us. Among the influences which have swayed our generation is not science dominant? Watching the scope and magnitude of our inventions, their determinant power over our future has seemed indubitable. A century ago Philip Hone, writing his diary in New York City, exclaimed exultantly: "We run faster, sail smarter, dive deeper and fly farther than any other people on the face of the earth." Philip Hone had taken his first trip on a railroad train from New York to Washington at the thrilling pace of thirty miles an hour. Steamships had actually crossed the ocean under their own power, and landed safely in New

York Harbor. A man in Cincinnati had completed a successful balloon trip. In New York University, Morse had demonstrated that the electric telegraph would work. The doors were opening on a glorious utopia, and for a century, filled with astounding scientific exploits, we Americans especially have continued in much the boastful mood of Philip Hone.

I am only in my seventies, but think what I have seen! The first bicylce factory in the United States was organized when I was minus one year old. The first telephone exchange in the United States with twenty-one subscribers was set up in New Haven, Connecticut, the year that I was born. Edison produced his electric light when I was one year old. It was in the year I graduated from college that Wilbur Wright wrote to his father that he was going to a place called Kitty Hawk, in North Carolina, to try a little experiment. "It is my belief," he said, "that flight is possible. I think there is a slight possibility of achieving fame and fortune from it." What a stupendous generation of scientific invention ours has been! Has that saved the world? All this new power in the hands of a human race whose ethical character and spiritual culture are no match for their technical civilization—has that redeemed us? Rather, as another put it: "The road to hell is paved with good *inventions*."

Our generation's confusion is due, in part, to this collapse of our reliance on the magnificent achievements of science. So a professor of physics in one of our state universities writes: "I have come to three conclusions: the first is that salvation is not to be found in science; secondly, we must have a moral revival; thirdly, we can have no moral revival without a living religion." That insight the world needs today. The greater the power we possess the more it demands ethical control. Our doom or blessing lies deep in the spiritual quality of men and women, and like a great bell tolls the word of Jesus: What shall it profit to gain the whole world and lose the soul?

This collapse of old reliances, however, despite

the consequent disillusionment, spells opportunity.
Stop being obsessed by size, it says; stop worship-
ing the colossal or letting the colossal frighten you!
Your hope is in vital persons, ideas, groups. In the
long run the future belongs to them. International,
economic, racial problems are immense, and everything we care for most depends on their solution;
but the solution of every gigantic problem is already here, almost imperceptible it may be, in some
inspired person, some germinative idea, some leavening group. And when such vitalities seem weak,
as in the face of our prodigious problems they
often do seem weak, we need to refresh our insight
concerning their possibilities. They are like Marquis wheat, now harvested by millions of bushels;
but once all the Marquis wheat in the world could
have been put into one envelope.

One readily can guess the retorts and objections
which such a statement as we have made may call
forth. Says one: You have talked as though the

vitalities were always good; but communism, for example, possesses powerful vitality not for good but for evil—ideals, ideas, faiths, loyalties, claiming devotion from millions and threatening the whole earth. That ominous fact is true, but it only emphasizes our theme's importance. This earth today is a battlefield of clashing ideas and faiths. *That* is the level on which the struggle must ultimately be waged and decided. The fight is not so much between one colossus and another, as between conflicting sets of ideas and faiths, and on that level military might is not decisive. You cannot kill an idea with a bomb; you must kill an idea with an idea. You cannot shoot a faith to death; you must supersede it with a faith. This is the nub of the whole matter—that the world's hope depends on vital persons, ideas, groups, representing the best and not the worst.

Another objection to our theme goes deeper. On a transient planet, someone says, vitality is not *ultimately* mightier than size. In the end the planet perishes, burned up by an exploding sun or frozen

out by a sun grown cold, and then where are all
these spiritual vitalities whose superior power you
sing? That objection is so serious that it requires
the whole Christian philosophy to meet it. He who
holds the Christian faith about this transient earth
alone is not holding the Christian faith. This
planet is temporary; once uninhabitable, it will.be
uninhabitable again; if it alone is the scene of God's
operation, then in the end the physical will certainly obliterate the spiritual and everything in the
solar universe will be as though no soul had ever
been at all.

This is the tragedy of atheism: it sees annihila-
tion awaiting every decent, creative, spiritual idea
and purpose on our planet. Atheism's ultimate
outlook is inescapable: "On man and all his race
the slow sure doom falls pitiless and dark." If our
theme is to be finally sustained, therefore, it must
be set in the wider context of the Christian faith.
Man's spiritual vitality is a revelation of the
Eternal. The best in us springs from the deepest
in Reality. Even a perishing planet, therefore, can-

not destroy it. "What is excellent," cried Emerson, "as God lives, is permanent."

Despite hell and high water, therefore, we Christians still put our faith in the vital as against the merely huge. In A.D. 156 Polycarp, a Christian martyr, was put to death in Smyrna, and the small struggling Christian community was terrified by the persecution under the proconsulship of Statius Quadratus, and was heartbroken by its leader's death. The man who wrote the record of it, however, for the centuries to read, boiled down a great truth into a few words when he dated the event. "Statius Quadratus, proconsul," he wrote, "Jesus Christ, king forever." I wonder if he guessed that in the twentieth century we should be reading that. Who was "Statius Quadratus, proconsul"? Long since sunk in oblivion! But still above the world's turmoil the affirmation resounds: "Jesus Christ, king forever!" That is a faith for tough times.

III

Adequate Power Is Available

Unbalanced budgets anywhere are deplorable, but in troubled times like these unbalanced budgets inside human souls are an especially grave calamity. Many persons today are spiritually insolvent. Life demands from them more than their resources can supply. Like exhausted reservoirs in a drought, whose constant expenditure is unbalanced by adequate replenishment, they run dry.

This disaster is sometimes seen in earnest Christians who eagerly accept that aspect of Christianity which calls for active service and who live busy, energetic lives, endlessly devoted to good works, like the women Jonathan Swift described, who, said he, "out of zeal for religion have hardly time to say their prayers." Others who suffer this calamity of inward exhaustion are anything but Christian, like the prodigal son, wasting his substance in riotous living until, not financially alone but spiritually too, as Jesus said, "when he had spent all he began to be in want." Still others suffer this disaster of a depleted soul mainly because they live in this grim, frustrating generation. One of the best-loved men in America in recent years was Ernie Pyle, a brave man, a great reporter, a warm-hearted friend. But all the more because we liked him so, one notes a repeated refrain in what he said. "There is no sense to the struggle," he wrote, "but there is no choice but to struggle." And again, "It seemed to me that living is futile, and death the final indignity." And again, "My wholly hopeless feeling about everything." And again, "I wish you would shine any of your light in my direction. God knows I've run out of light." A disillusioning era like ours can do *that* to a fine man.

Budgets can sometimes be balanced by reduction of expenditure, and there are doubtless overzealous souls who need that. They undertake too much, assume too weighty responsibilities, overextend themselves. Our generation, however, demands heavy output from decent folk. In such an era one cannot conscientiously live unburdened by mankind's agony and doing nothing about it. Let those reduce expenditure who need to! Most of us, if ever we are to balance our budgets, must increase our income.

Any faith fitted for tough times, therefore, involves a gospel of available power for daily living. Jesus, seeing his disciples overstrained and fatigued, called them away to replenish in solitude their spent resources. Without *that* nothing notable could have come from the hard-driven group of his first followers. They found through him wide margins of reserve around their daily need, and deep wells to draw their strength and courage from. They learned the secret, without which Christian living at its best is forever impossible:

> Lord, what a change within us one short hour
> Spent in Thy presence, will prevail to make!

At the vital center of the Christian life is this divine-human encounter, this direct access of the soul to God, from which inward reënforcement comes, and with it confidence that whether in personal living or in social tasks adequate power is available.

So Ezekiel, exiled in Babylon, cried, "The Spirit entered into me . . . and set me upon my feet." So the Psalmist, facing evildoers who came upon him to eat up his flesh, wrote, "The Lord is my light and my salvation; whom shall I fear? The Lord is the strength of my life; of whom shall I be afraid?" So Isaiah, confronting national disaster, said, "They that wait upon the Lord shall renew their strength." So Paul, facing situations which would have defeated most of us, found his dependable reliance—"strengthened with might through His Spirit in the inner man."

For such men religion was not simply a creed about God, but an intimate relationship with God; not simply theistic theory but personal experience of an environing Presence, whence the soul draws courage and strength. Such faith takes for granted the tragedy of human life, the sin and stupidity of man and the catastrophic turmoil of nations. It is founded, not on the niceness of the world, but on inward awareness of adequate power to confront the world, despite devilish men and hellish circumstance.

Our serious need of this Biblical experience is lighted up when we watch the attitudes of those who lack it.

Some are rebellious, shaking their fists in the face of an antagonistic universe. So, after the funeral service for her only son, a mother said to me: "It is all right! It is all right! He is well out of this damned world." That mother, far from triumphant, was defiant, challenging even a hostile cosmos to make her cringe.

Others mount the judgment seat and vent their righteous indignation on this wicked world. So Mark Twain once wrote to a friend of his: "I have been reading the morning paper. I do it every morning—well knowing that I shall find in it the usual depravities and basenesses and hypocrisies and cruelties that make up civilization, and cause me to put in the rest of the day pleading for the damnation of the human race." Such a mood may exhibit a righteous and useful conscience but, by itself alone, it reveals no constructive power.

Others try stoic indifference to the meaninglessness of the universe, determined nonetheless to get the most out of it, whatever its purposeless nature and futile outcome. So one modern says that a wise man can regard life as "comedy, or high tragedy, or plain farce," and can still enjoy it. One salutes his buoyant spirit, but if comedy, tragedy and farce sum up life's meaning, one knows that the profoundest experiences of the human soul go unaccounted for, and the noblest faiths that have sustained our race have the ground cut out from under them.

Others decide to disregard superhuman reliance, to let theism and atheism fight it out and, with no faith concerning what Reality is, to center attention and endeavor on what man ought to be and do. One applauds the fine spirit of this brave attempt, but still the conviction will not down that, in the long run, the eternal truth about this cosmos cannot so lightly be brushed off; that the *ought* depends upon the *is* both for its ideals and for the power to make their fulfilment possible. What is really *so* about this universe is the determiner of destiny for every hope man sets his heart upon.

Others candidly acknowledge life's futility without superhuman resources, and confess their frustration and bewilderment. "Is this, then, all that life amounts to?" asks one of them. "To stumble, almost by mistake, into a universe that clearly was not designed for life and which, to all appearances, is either totally indifferent or definitely hostile to it, to stay clinging on to a fragment of a grain of sand until we are frozen off, to strut our tiny hour on our tiny stage with the knowledge that our aspirations are all doomed to final frustration, and that our achievements must perish with our race, leaving the universe as though we had never been." To which the Christian answers: Well, *is* this, then, all that life amounts to?

Such attitudes commonly characterize those who

lack a profoundly personal religious faith. Defiant; indignant; trying to make the best of a senseless existence; promoting goodness in a world where goodness, it may be, is an accidental intruder; or frankly frustrated and cynical—such states of mind are familiar now. Over against them consider a man who had tapped resources of power from beyond himself. He, too, lived in a frustrating era. He himself was in a Roman prison. He knew all about mankind's desperate predicament. But he wrote this: "I know how to be abased, and I know how to abound; in any and all circumstances I have learned the secret of facing plenty and hunger, abundance and want. I can do all things in him who strengthens me."

That such resourceful character is desirable is evident but, say some, this experience of superhuman reënforcement demands confident faith, and how does a man get that, if he lacks it? He cannot blow upon his hands and hoist himself into a belief which to his intellect seems incredible. Confronting this honest difficulty, one must grant that, of course, the experience of divine resource demands faith. Yet, what if the relationship between faith and experience is a two-way street? What if it is not only true that faith leads to experience, but also true that experience leads to faith? Remember that haunting sentence of Canon Streeter: "I have had experiences which materialism cannot explain." *That* is the origin of the most victorious faith in Christian history—not credulous acceptance of dogma, not docile subservience to ecclesiastical authority, but a veritable, firsthand encounter with spiritual reality, sometimes unsought and unwanted, which convinces even an unwilling mind that something more than human power is operating here. So Hugh Walpole described his experience: "I affirm that I have become aware, not by my own wish, almost against my will, of the existence of another life of far, far greater importance and beauty than this physical one."

Such an experience is the germinative kernel of vital religion. Creeds come and go, churches rise and fall, theological arguments lose cogency and must be rephrased, but ever the human soul at its best experiences invading spiritual forces which can transform, illumine, direct and empower life. When Joseph Wood Krutch writes, "The inevitable realization that living is merely a physiological process with only a physiological meaning," he states the inescapable logic of atheism, but the profound experiences of the human soul rise up to deny it. Living is not merely a physiological process. Man's spirit can be too plainly reënforced by more than human resources for that to be true.

Man has an inborn capacity to be inspired. As a ship in a lock is lifted, not by what the ship does but by what it receives—the inpouring of water from above—so our spirits can be raised by an influx from beyond ourselves, until upon a higher level they sail out again.

Man has an inborn capacity for worship. We are made not simply to look down but to look up, and healing hours of restoration come when, in receptive reverence and awe, we "love the highest when we see it."

Man has an inborn capacity for spiritual companionship. Our souls are homes where we can welcome guests, unseen but real, in whose fellowship we find peace and power. Not rare mystics only, but every genuinely Christian soul knows what the hymn means:

> Thou Life within my life, than self more near,
> Thou veiléd Presence, infinitely clear,
> From all illusive shows of sense I flee,
> To find my center and my rest in Thee.

Man has an inborn capacity to experience transforming invasions of power that make life all over. Bodies are born but once; souls can be reborn. So one young man who came to me in moral disaster saying, "I do not believe in God but, if you do, for God's sake pray for me, for I need it," exclaimed after a victory which his unaided strength never could have won: "If ever you find a man who does not believe in God, send him to me. I know."

Man has an inborn capacity to be a channel of spiritual dynamic from beyond himself. The great souls have done their work, feeling that it was being done not so much by them as through them. They were not cisterns, but artesian wells. Cisterns cannot stand some things—drought, rainless months when the skies are brass—but an artesian well, facing all that, is unexhausted still, amid parched fields and failing reservoirs, replenished from hidden depths.

Life merely a physiological process—not faith alone, but fact denies that. Here is the root and origin of vital religion: the soul has experiences which materialism cannot explain.

This, then, is a faith for tough times: *Just as around our bodies is a physical world from which we draw our physical strength, so around our spirits is a Spiritual Environment, with which we can live in vital contact, and from which we can draw replenishing power.* He who understands that has

entered into the profoundest experience of the
Christian life. Paul described it when he said,
"The spirit of God dwelleth in you." Jesus called it
going into the closet, shutting the door, and praying to the Father who seeth in secret. Boutroux,
the French philosopher, called it, "the Beyond that
is within, with which man comes in touch on the
inner side of his nature." Tennyson called it contact with

... that true world, within the world we see,
Whereof our world is but the bounding shore.

Call it what you will, the reality of this enriching
experience has behind it the confident testimony of
our race's greatest souls, and of numberless humble
folk who have lived in the power of it.

How do we gain assurance that the physical
world is real? We do not start with faith and
deduce from it the experience of the outer world's
veritable presence; we rather start with experience
and so gain confidence that the physical is real.
Fulfilling conditions in the physical realm, we

obtain appropriate results. That experience, generation after generation, makes it certain that the physical is real. It must be; it responds to us; our proper action evokes an answering action; something substantial must be there. So faith in the spiritual world's reality is not faith alone. It begins with factual experience. Fulfilling spiritual conditions we are answered with spiritual results. Agelong and timeless across the centuries that testimony runs. The soul does not cry into emptiness and hear only an echo. An answer comes, often with transforming consequence. Spiritual hospitality finds a guest waiting to come in. The opened window lets in light from beyond itself. Exhausted spirits are reënforced; whipped souls become more than conquerors; seers and saints, prophets and apostles, are empowered for leadership. Faith in the reality of the spiritual world is not a leap in the dark, but a conviction often forced on our unwilling minds by the soul's experience.

Our generation has not stressed this similarity between assurance of an extrahuman physical world and confidence in a superhuman spiritual realm, but has strongly emphasized the differences between them. Granted the differences—the physical world visible, tangible, metric; the spiritual world invisible, intangible, nonmetric. Nevertheless, our experience of the one is just as factual and real as our experience of the other. Absorbed in the beauty of a Beethoven symphony, one is even more certain of that experience than of the physical scientist's accuracy in counting the air waves or stating the theory of sound. So, not only to mystics, but to multitudes of plain folk, the most convincing experiences in life have been the soul's encounters with divine reality. Frederick Myers rightly reports the testimony of multitudes, when he represents Paul as saying,

> Whoso has felt the Spirit of the Highest
> Cannot confound nor doubt Him nor deny:
> Yea with one voice, O world, tho' thou deniest,
> Stand thou on that side, for on this am I.

But, runs the familiar objection, in the physical realm accurate verification is possible, while in the spiritual realm the vast affirmations of religious faith are incapable of any such metric demonstration. Undoubtedly that contrast is true, but it is commonly exaggerated. The physical cosmos, too, is profoundly mysterious, and the farther one moves out toward ultimate explanations, the more one leaves neat and tidy verification behind, and deals with hypotheses beyond the reach of demonstration. Lately I heard one of our leading biologists tell a group of his colleagues that biologists at present do not really understand a single basic biological reaction. One would suppose that physicists must know what light is, but there are, in fact, two theories of light, and which is true has not been proved. One physicist even remarks that laboratories use one theory on Mondays, Wednesdays and Fridays, and the other on Tuesdays, Thursdays and Saturdays. As for the innermost secrets of the cosmos, Professor Jeans says: "The ultimate realities of the universe are at present quite beyond the reach of science, and may be— and probably are—forever beyond the comprehension of the human mind." The physical realm, too, is unfathomably mysterious, as is the spiritual. Nevertheless, despite conflicting theories and unproved hypotheses, man's agelong experience, backed by the best thinking of which he is capable, confirms one thing for sure—the physical is real, and in dealing with it we handle substantial fact.

So a wise Christian is humble about his theology. Our theories concerning the spiritual world are partial, incomplete, like a picture puzzle only a little worked out. What more can a man expect of mortal mind in this inscrutably mysterious universe? But nonetheless all is not dubiousness and uncertainty, a mere "grand Perhaps," as Browning's Bishop Blougram called it. Our interpretations of the spiritual world are diverse, imperfect, erroneous. "At present," as Paul said, "we see only the baffling reflections in a mirror." But that does not prevent, in the spiritual any more than in the physical realm, a profound certainty, grounded in experience: the spiritual world is real; we can thrust our roots into it and draw sustenance from it; our souls have an unseen Friend, an invisible Companion; as Jesus said, "I am not alone, but I and my Father."

Moreover, the scientist's confidence in and alliance with the physical realm have no monopoly on the kind of verification supplied by practical results. Momentous consequences also follow vital faith in and coalition with the spiritual world. John Wesley's conversion issued in a religious and ethical revolution which, says J. R. Green, the English historian, "changed in a few years the whole temper of English society." To relegate to the realm of fantasy, illusion and self-deception all the transformed lives, the reënforced characters and the inspired leadership whose fountainhead was faith in the reality of God and in his available power requires more credulity than most of us can attain to. Such substantial results argue a substantial reality from which they spring. Any way one looks at the matter, our confidence in the reality of the physical and our confidence in the reality of the spiritual stand on much the same ground.

Ours is a generation that tries men's souls. Nervous ailments multiply; character breaks down; hope fails and faith goes to pieces. In such a generation a sensitive soul experiences Gethsemane. In fortunate days we do not easily identify ourselves with Jesus' tragic struggle in the Garden, but in these grim times, how can a Christian stay out of it? "If it be possible," cried the Master, "let this cup pass from me." Who now can help praying *that*? A third world war, the collapse of Europe and Asia under Soviet armies, the destruction of civilization by H-bombs—if it be possible, let this cup pass from me! The militarization of our own country, the mobilization of our children and grandchildren, the cancelation of the magnificent possibilities of peaceful progress as we become monsters in order to fight a monster—if it be possible, let this cup pass from me! Then add personal anxieties and disasters which we pray to escape, and the Garden of Gethsemane is not remote from any of us.

I visited that Garden once—outwardly. There on the Mount of Olives under the olive trees I stood, and saw the evening shadows close down over the landscape our Lord's eyes had rested on. While my mood was reverent, however, and my sympathy warm, I was not really in the Garden then. But now sometimes I am. After two world wars I would far rather die than see another. For our children and grandchildren my troubled petition rises that they may not be struck down by the perils which threaten us. One way or another, who can help offering the Master's Gethsemane prayer: "If it be possible . . ."?

What was it that enabled him to utter that next word: "Nevertheless"? "O my Father," he cried, "if it be possible, let this cup pass from me: *nevertheless* not as I will, but as thou wilt." Few greater words than that are in man's vocabulary. In agony our Lord foresaw the cross—nevertheless! His tortured spirit cried for escape—nevertheless! What is the spiritual resource which enables a man in Gethsemane to utter that momentous word?

For one thing, such a soul has a reassuring background for his life. Foreground and background—those two make up our experience. The foreground is the immediate business of life, its work and play, its personal relationships and preoccupying tasks, its obsessing problems amid the world's confusion. Upon these foreground affairs most of our conscious thought is expended; but ever and again we raise our eyes and see life's background. There it stands, filling the horizon like hills around a plain—not something we constantly deal with or, it may be, commonly think about, but always there, the setting and matrix of our lives.

To many people—although they may not have analyzed their trouble—this is the real problem now. When come their moments of release from the immediate and they think, as everyone at times must think, of life's background, what they see is a purposeless universe, hostile to man's best hopes and ideals, or at least indifferent, a cosmos empty of reassurance and reënforcement for mankind. They work hard, fall in love, enjoy the symphony and theater, fill their days with business, and do their duty as citizens, but then comes the inevitable pause when their thought drifts to the background, and there looms the vast, formidable, forbidding, spiritually empty universe.

The devastating consequences of this experience are obvious. It is bad enough to have the foreground in chaos, but when the background also is ominous and dreadful, no wonder nervous breakdowns multiply! No wonder disillusionment and cynicism flourish! No wonder moral standards collapse and men cry, What's the use!

In contrast, the first effect of the Christian experience, which we have been endeavoring to state, concerns life's background—so conceiving it that, though the foreground be dismaying, the soul can face it with a triumphant *Nevertheless.*

To suppose that we Christians go about all day consciously thinking of God, meditating on the great affirmations of our faith, remembering Christ and looking forward to immortality, would be sheer pretense. We do no such thing. We are just as preoccupied as anyone else with daily tasks. But when the pause comes—that inevitable moment when one's eyes are raised from the immediate— not depression but exultation follows. "I will lift up mine eyes unto the hills, from whence cometh my help," sang the Psalmist out of a troubled foreground, but encouraged and empowered whenever he looked up. The hills whence his help came— they were his background. Such was the secret of the Master's victory in his Gethsemane.

The Master's triumph, however, sprang from factors far more intimate than anything the word "background" can connote. We have used the phrase "spiritual world" to describe the environing Presence that surrounds men's souls. But nothing

spiritual exists outside the realm of the personal.
Avoiding anthropomorphism as best we can, and
humbly confessing the insufficiency of any words,
drawn from human life, to describe the divine,
it still remains true that a spiritual world must be
personal. It is not simply a "world"; it is God—a
God of moral purpose, his creation not finished
yet, calling men into alliance to complete it, com-
missioning them with divine vocations, entrusting
them with causes everlastingly right to which they
must be loyal though the heavens fall and supply-
ing them with adequate power to carry on.

A reassuring background did sustain the Master
in his Gethsemane but, deeper yet, the experience
of inner replenishment from inexhaustible resources. He was no cistern, but an artesian well.
So, though he prayed with bloody sweat that he
might escape the cross—nevertheless! Who here
is not tempted to stop the Master's prayer short of
that triumphant word? "If it be possible, let this
cup pass from me"—period! To go on from there,
to face the worst that life can do to us, to confront

the misery, iniquity, barbaric cruelty and chaotic confusion of our times with a resounding "Nevertheless," and to tackle our problems and the world's problems with undefeated faith and determination—that calls for inner reserves of power, enabling a man to rise every morning sure that nothing can happen to him which God and he together cannot handle, so that what he ought to do he can do and what he must endure he can stand.

So far we have been thinking of this religion of direct divine-human encounter, of inner personal reënforcement from superhuman resources, in contrast with the irreligion of unbelievers. Even more important is it, however, for Christians to face the contrast between such firsthand religion and the secondhand religion which afflicts our churches.

Church membership in this nation is at an all-time high. Never, in recent years, has so large a proportion of our population been inside the churches. Church attendance is apparently increasing, and 95 per cent of our people, poll-takers say, believe in God. Yet, look at us! In one realm after another of personal and public behavior we do not give the impression to ourselves or to anybody else that we are really a Christian people.

To be sure, while there are more than eighty-five million members of Christian churches and Jewish synagogues, there are more millions of our population outside. Nevertheless, we cannot put all the blame on them. Eighty-five million professed servants of God and members of his organized fellowship ought to be making more difference than we are making. Something inside the churches is wrong, and one aspect of that wrong is obvious: millions of our church members are secondhand Christians. Their Christianity is formal, not vital; they have inherited it from their families, borrowed it from their friends, taken it over like the cut of their clothes from the fashion of their group. Their churchmanship is part of their respectability—not hypocritically professed, they believe it after a fashion; but the profound experiences of the Christian soul, which transform character, sustain strength and courage, dedicate life, and make God personally real, they have not known at firsthand. They are Christians by hearsay rather than by vital, inward apprehension and insight.

All of us necessarily start with secondhand religion. We hear about Christian faith and life before we experience it; in family and church we accept its expressions before we vitally see for ourselves its meaning. As we hear, and in a way believe, that Beethoven is a great musician before we are inwardly, intimately captivated by him, so in every important realm secondhand acceptance precedes firsthand experience. Many, however, in their Christianity never pass over that momentous boundary line between hearsay and personal insight. They never, like Job, have said to God: "I had heard of Thee by the hearing of the ear; but now mine eye seeth Thee." From traditional acceptance to vital apprehension, from believing in general that religion is a good thing to being transformed by an inward encounter with the divine which makes God's presence and power one's very own—if all secondhand Christians should thus become firsthand Christians, the results would be revolutionary.

There are three major reasons why secondhand Christianity flourishes.

First, much of our religion comes to us by inheritance. As with great literature, as with our democracy, so with our Christianity, we are not its first inspired pioneers; we did not create it. It comes to us as a heritage from our forefathers and, in a way, we can so accept it, taking over from family, Bible and church the religious tradition. We may even marry it, and like many a man may hold our religion in our wife's name—not with conscious insincerity, but formally accepting Christ as many accept Shakespeare, a great literary heritage in whose supreme genius they believe, but about whose works they do not for themselves know or care much of anything at all. He never did any-thing intimate to them. How much Christianity in our churches means no more than that!

Some things can be outwardly inherited. Real estate—we can merely take it over. Railroads, automobiles, electric lights—we can start using them. But all the courage of the past means noth-ing to a man who cannot say, "My courage." All the prayer of the past cannot nourish the soul that never prayed, "Spirit of God, descend upon my heart." All the transformed lives in Christian his-tory will not redeem anyone who cannot say, "One thing I know, that, whereas I was blind, now I see." In these deep, vital realms there are no proxies for the soul. As Goethe said, "The posses-sions which you have inherited from your an-cestors—*earn* them in order truly to *own* them."

Another reason for the prevalence of second-hand Christianity is that we commonly get at our faith by argument. Once Napoleon Bonaparte, crossing the Mediterranean on a clear night, heard one of his military officers question the existence of God. Napoleon waved his hand toward the stars and said, "Who then made the constellations?" He knew the arguments; he accepted them; he believed in God. But what difference did that make to Napoleon himself, his character, his ambitions, his personal quality? "If any man is in Christ, he is a new creature"; "He that loveth, abideth in God and God abideth in him"—Napoleon knew nothing about such firsthand experiences as that. His religion was only secondhand belief.

An old proverb says, "Seeing is believing." Yes, but the reverse is not true; believing is not necessarily seeing. Believing can be superficial, passive acceptance of something never experienced at all. Some of us believed for years that the Yosemite Valley is beautiful but, then, one day we saw. Some of us long believed that a happy home with children and grandchildren gathered around one's aging years was above all life's experiences the loveliest, but then came the time when we knew it for ourselves. Some of us, like tourists with Baedeker in hand, looking at the great souls of the race,

long believed that God could inwardly sustain a
man in trouble, but then the day came when we
walked through the valley of the shadow of death
and feared no evil for God was with us. Believing
is not necessarily seeing; believing can be merely
formal, conventional acquiescence. Of all the 95
per cent of our population professing faith in God,
how many do you think are only secondhand be-
lievers, who never have known at firsthand God's
inward, sustaining, cleansing, dedicating presence?

For still another reason, especially potent in our
time, secondhand Christianity is prevalent. We
are publicly confronted now with the opposite of
Christianity—atheism rampant, made into a political creed by communism, menacing the whole
world with deliberate anti-Christian propaganda.
That combination of atheism, communism, and
Russian totalitarianism frightens all of us, threatening everything we hold most dear. Is not the
growth in our church membership and attendance,
and the rising determination of our people that
the spiritual values of our religious heritage shall

be taught to our children, due in large measure to this political peril we face? Sometimes on a small film we cannot easily discern the details of a picture, or get its perspective and range, but when we put it into the projectoscope and cast it on the screen, then we can see its meaning. So anti-Christianity, thought of privately, we might be indifferent about, but now it is cast upon the vast screen of the world for all to see. Millions of Americans are reacting indignantly against this public paganism, this organized atheism, this barbaric anti-Christianity, and begin to think that they had better be counted on the Christian side.

That is good as far as it goes, but you see the kind of secondhand Christianity it can issue in. Being a Christian for political reasons does not carry anyone into the profundities of the gospel. It can lead one to attend church, to send one's children to Church School, to contribute to the church's budget, to say that American Christianity is far better than Russian anti-Christianity, but it still can leave a man in the environs of Christian faith and life with no inward firsthand experience of God's saving grace in Christ. And when, let us suppose, the Russian menace is removed, what then? Why then we can slip back into indifference again. Christian faith and life have not been to us our inward sustenance and strength, our personal victory over the world, our intimate possession, our salvation and our hope.

When we think of conversion we commonly think of downright wicked people born again into upright character, of prodigals in the Far Country turning homeward, of drunkards rescued from alcoholism, and debauchees transformed by the renewing of their minds. Another kind of conversion is also needed now—decent church members who never doubted Christianity, for years acquiescent about it, respectful toward it, formally believing in it, who suddenly make a great discovery: this means *me*—inwardly and intimately it means *me*—a resource of spiritual power, overcoming fear, renewing courage, directing conscience, dedicating life. It is more than a great tradition, more than passively accepted belief, more than political loyalty—it is my personal victory that overcometh the world. "O God," cried the Psalmist, "O God, Thou art my God."

The trouble with secondhand religion in days like these is practical. It will not stand up when the storm breaks on us. In tough times when personal grief, overwhelming temptation, moral failure, public calamity land on us, secondhand religion lets us down. We want more than a tradition then, more than passively accepted belief, more than an idea that Christianity is better than communism. We want an experience of God in Christ that is our very own. "God," said Emerson, "enters by a private door into every individual." That is the religion we want when we face life's profoundest need. Sometimes Paul called his faith *the* gospel; "the gospel of God," . . . "the gospel of Christ," he said. But sometimes he writes, "*my* gospel." That is what saw Paul through. Not just the gospel, my gospel! That is the kind of Christianity which can stand the gaff in times like these.

"Strengthened with might by his Spirit in the inner man"—do we know what that means? God, even when believed in, can be as far off as the rings of Saturn. Like Napoleon's deity, he merely made the constellations. But God can be like a well underground in a man's soul; as Jesus said to the woman of Samaria, "The water that I shall give him shall become in him a well of water springing up." Do we know that God—not just a theory to explain the universe, but available inward resource as real as water, as real as bread, sustaining the spirit in the darkest days that fall. That is firsthand religion.

Or, remember Elijah facing wind, earthquake and fire and finding God in none of them. "And after the fire a still small voice. And it was so, when Elijah heard it, that he wrapped his face in his mantle, and went out, and stood." Do we know what that means? In this uproarious era wind, earthquake and fire are obvious, but God pity the man who sees and hears nothing else! Once during the Civil War, when things were at their worst, the Governor of Illinois wrote Abraham Lincoln an utterly discouraged letter—everything going to the dogs! And Lincoln wrote back: "Dear Dick: Stand still and see the salvation of the Lord." From Moses who said that first, from Elijah and his still small voice, from the Psalmist, "Be still and know that I am God," to Lincoln is a long haul, but continuous experience unites them. In their uproarious days such men could at times be silent and listen; and in the silence was a voice—guidance, insight, reassurance, divine alliance—so that from the silence they went forth to stand their ground, though this world with devils filled should threaten to undo them. That is firsthand religion.

Or "We must obey God rather than men"— do we know what that means? God, theoretically believed in, can have as little practical influence on daily living as the man in the moon. To cry "Lord, Lord," as Jesus said, with no ethical consequence, is easy. So one of our poets sarcastically describes worshipers in church:

They do it every Sunday,
They'll be all right on Monday;
It's just a little habit they've acquired.

But God, the eternal good, the magnetic pole of everlasting righteousness which, though it be transcendent and cosmic, sways every compass needle in every ship that sails the sea, and is to be obeyed despite wind and wave—that is another matter. That means conscientiousness. That means rectitude and integrity, whatever the fashions of the time. "What this parish needs, needs before everything else," cried Thomas Carlyle, "is a preacher who knows God otherwise than by hearsay." That is the whole world's need. "To go against one's conscience is neither safe nor right," said Luther. "Here I stand. I cannot do otherwise. God help me! Amen!" That is firsthand religion.

Or, recall Isaiah hearing a divine voice crying, "Whom shall I send, and who will go for us?" and Isaiah said, "Here am I; send me." Do we know what that means? In vital personal religion every man is commissioned with his vocation, called to do something, big or little, for God's sake and man's. The real God is Purpose, hard at work getting something done on earth to redeem our race from its sin and misery, calling every man to some task which, in the place where he is put, no one can do in his stead. "Here am I; send me," said Isaiah. "I was not disobedient unto the heavenly vision," said Paul. That is firsthand religion.

Ah, Church of Christ, the proclamation of such faith is your task today. You fritter away your strength on trivial sectarianisms. You insult the intelligent and alienate the serious with petty dogmatisms that do not matter. You fiddle trifling tunes while the world burns. But back of all that, still the glory of the true church within the church, is a message without which mankind is doomed. If you really believe the Christian gospel—God behind us, his cause committed to us, his power available for us—then proclaim it, live it, implement it, for humanity's hope depends upon it. It is, indeed, a faith for tough times.

Index

Index

Index

Life: background of, 107-9; emerging complexity of, 60; final significance of, 14; foreground of, 107, 109; meaninglessness of, 13, 15-16; unchanging purpose of, 11

Lincoln, Abraham, quoted, 122

Love, 33; of God, 40

Lowell, James Russell, quoted, 36

Luther, quoted, 67, 123

MacArthur, Douglas, quoted, 70

Man: capacity of, for nonmaterial experiences, 96-98; mind of, 25-26; perfectibility of, 29, 30; revelation of Eternal in, 83

Materialism, 26, 42; limitation of, 95, 98

Mathematics, 19, 20, 23, 26

Mind of man, 25-26; emergence of, 60; as eternal truth, 27

Militarization, 105

Moffatt, James, 62

Mommsen, quoted, 34

Moral customs, instability of, 12, 35

Moral law, eternal, 34-40

Moses, 122

Myers, Frederick, quoted, 101

Napoleon, 39, 66, 67, 115-16

Nebuchadnezzar, 56

Needs, different, for different generations, 14-15, 27

Newton, Isaac, 42, 59

Niebuhr, Reinhold, quoted, 72

"One world," 17, 54, 55

Optimism, 28-29, 30, 31, 54

Paul, 67; distinction of, between fleeting and abiding, 32-33; faith of, 18-19; quoted, 99, 101, 103, 120, 124; personal gospel of, 120; reliance of, on power beyond himself, 90, 94

Penn, William, 22

Perfectibility of man, 29, 30

Permanent, 21-22; necessity for finding, 15-19

Personality, 33, 40-44, 56, 65; centrality of, 27; vitality of, 56-65

Philosophies, 25-26

Physical world: mysteriousness of, 102-3; reality of, 99-100, 103, 104

Polycarp, 84

Power: available, gospel of, 89-91; capacity to experience, 97; ethics and, 80; inner reserves of, 97, 110, 111

Practicality, 58-59

Priesthood, Jewish, 18

Prodigal son, 87

Progress: inevitable, idea of, 28-29, 30; material, 20-21, 78-80

Protoplasm vs. volcanoes, 51

Purpose, eternal, 28-34

Pyle, Ernie, on meaninglessness of life, 88

Ra, 68

Rationalists, 29-30

Rauschenbusch, Walter, quoted, 30

Rebellion against universe, 91

Reënforcement, inward, 89-90, 100, 110, 111

Religion: attitudes of those lacking, 91-94; confidence in, shaken, 11; dereliction of, 75-78, 112, 113-19, 120, 124; and experiences of the soul, 96-98; firsthand, 111, 121-24; inherited, 114; involving relationship with God, 90-91; profoundest meaning of, 11; revelation of the unshakable in, 16-17; secondhand, 112, 113-19, 120

Responsibility, relief from, 33

Revolution, 52-53; religious and ethical, 104

Index